LABYRINTHS

LABYRINTHS

Kevin M. Cahill, M.D.

Refuge Press, New York, 2020

Fordham University IHA Book Series

ISBN #13: 978-0-8232-9365-0
All royalties from this book go to the training of humanitarian workers.

First printing 2019
Second printing, revised 2020

Printed in the United States of America.

For the people of Point Lookout

Acknowledgements

While many of the reflections in this brief memoir long predate the International Humanitarian Affairs (IHA) Book Series, it provides a necessary foundation to understand the approach of this writer who is the Author or Editor of that series. I am grateful to those cited as influences at various stages of a most blessed life. The manuscript was typed–and re-typed, and re-typed–by Maria J. Aramanda, Esq., with professional skill and enormous good will. Mary Clare Cahill provided high resolution scans of the photos and images. The book jacket was designed by Mauro Sarri. My sons made helpful comments on the text, refreshing my memories and keeping the record accurate. Finally, in a serendipitous linking two favorite places on my journey of life, the title of this book emerged during a telephone conversation from my base in Point Lookout with a dear friend, Mounir Neamatalla, at his Eco-Lodge in the Siwa Oasis deep in the Western Desert of Egypt.

Table of Contents

Why Oh Why

Family lore indicates that I had a fiercely independent personality from early childhood. Obstacles were seen as transient challenges that would inevitably be overcome, and age or title barriers were mere irritants. If bluebirds could fly over rainbows why oh why shouldn't I explore the unknowns, and experience the unique joys of discovering new ways of seeing and dealing with the world. I was supported by a close family, wonderful teachers and mentors, professional colleagues, and, most important, by a loving partner who shared in every venture from our teenage years till her death in 2004.

After my wife Kate died, I made a list documenting service as a physician and/or humanitarian worker in 65 countries, almost all after natural disasters or in conflict zones. Kate came with me on followup trips to 45 refugee camps. Our marriage, one of rare heavenly bliss, was honed to perfection in difficult and often exotic settings. I cite these influences in the opening of a brief book aimed at defining my approach to establishing relief operations in the midst of chaos, and in creating training programs and an academic curriculum to help standardize an emerging discipline. As the University Professor and Director of the International Institute of Humanitarian Affairs (IIHA) at Fordham University in New York I am responsible for coordinated courses all around the world; we now have over 3000 graduates from 140 nations.

In academia, it is essential to have a formal record documenting training and experience in order to secure legitimacy, especially in creating foundations for a complex field such as international humanitarian assistance. Many of those building blocks are considered later in this book, but critical aspects of this formative process could be easily missed unless a memoir attempts to fill an important gap by defining the why and how of my own personal involvement.

The origins of my professional life can, I suggest, be found more accurately in the biographical vignettes offered here rather than in any courses attended in college or medical school. There simply was no focus on humanitarian assistance during my training, and lessons learned were part of a humbling "work in progress." In many ways these current reflections are the glue that can bind my earlier publications in this field into a cohesive body of knowledge. Drawing from an almost endless skein of memories, I have selected strands that can be woven into an individual tale of identity. Some experiences obviously shape us more than others, and I have chosen those from youth and early career that had a lasting impact throughout my life.

Who am I? How did I become this person, with my own unique way of seeing the world, defining goals, joys or sorrows? Why did I pursue certain passions, and be unmoved by other equally attractive and valid drives? How do I deal with success or failure, with everyday, mundane problems? What forces shape the way I analyze puzzlement, create, initiate, innovate, share, give, receive, protect, sublimate? Are there specific roots one can isolate from which one's strengths, weaknesses, or resiliency emerge? How far back does one have to go to find the origins of a persona?

We are all influenced in infancy and childhood by genetics, by the mores and customs of family. In my instance the story starts a generation before I was born, with all four grandparents emigrating from Ireland in poverty, but with dreams and determination. In those years they held a "wake" for the immigrant, as they might for the deceased, for when one left it was likely to be forever. They survived in the new world by a basic system of mutual ethnic support, and by adhering to the universal code of the outsider in society. An old Irish relative, in his policeman's uniform, warned me at the age of five, "Never write what you can say, and never say it if you can nod your head." That was an immigrant's way of avoiding conflict, so that his children would have an education and more secure life in America.

My father's father came to the United States as a young man from rural County Kerry. He had listed himself on the ship's roster as "scholar". He came through Ellis Island, was befriended by his cousin, Denis, a policeman, and within a few years joined the NYPD. Gradually, through the mounted horse corps, and the street patrol, he became a Captain; he was NYPD's first Director of the Telegraph Center, proudly supervising a handful of Morse code operators in a single, sparse room. I have a picture of him in that room in my Fifth Avenue desk drawer, never forgetting from whence I sprung.

His wife died in the childbirth of their third child, Catherine; and he raised his sons, Dan and John, and their daughter with devotion and skill, factors not uncommon in the American Irish immigrant. Since his sons went to a Jesuit scholarship school, it seemed natural to him, though in retrospect it must have been inordinately rare, that he learn Latin and Greek in order to check their homework. He died of diabetes four years before I was born, but his influence remained strong in our family.

My father's brother, Dan, had just become a practicing lawyer when the Great Depression hit America. My father had, simultaneously, begun medical school and could not afford the tuition (one of the framed items in my office is a 1930 bill from Georgetown Medical School: $350 for the semester with a $10 rental fee for a microscope). Dan gave up his legal career to become a public school teacher in order to secure a regular salary that could pay Dad's way through medical school, an act my father never forgot.

My mother's father and mother lived long enough for me to remember them as much as a five year old can recall the smells of an old man and woman. They moved into a house on the same block as us in the Bronx in order to be near my father's medical care. I recall little of this subdued, introspective couple. He was a "bookie", a person who set odds and accepted bets on horse races. Years later, I was proud to know he was remembered at the Saratoga Race Track as "Honest Mike."

My maternal grandmother's sister and brother-in-law both died of the "Spanish Flu" in 1919 leaving behind nine young children. "Honest Mike" adopted the family, raising them with his own eight children in a large house in Brooklyn. Those were pre-welfare days, and immigrants protected their own, out of love, loyalty, and necessity. They didn't expect praise, and probably didn't get much. They did whatever was required to keep the family together. All seventeen children graduated from college, no mean feat in any generation.

My earliest memories at about age four, of our home, are of a gentle, colorful, seemingly endless flowing pattern of almost predictable household tasks, affected by the seasons, the sea, and Celtic fairy tales. There were deeply ingrained, but not oppressive, religious traditions in our Irish Catholic home–nightly prayers, Saturday confession, Sunday Communion, First Fridays, Ash Wednesdays, with the symbolic markings of burnt palms on the forehead, Lenten sacrifices, Easter, the birth of the Baby Jesus, Sodality, the family rosary "disaster"–all gave a particular rhythm to the calendar year.

The family rosary was promoted by a cape-waving cleric on early TV under the adage "the family that prays together stays together." This particular spiritual exercise quickly collapsed in the Cahill home. Trying to keep eight young children on their knees after dinner, repeating prayers and counting beads, was doomed when my father's pants fell to his ankles as he rose to discipline an inattentive, playful boy. Laughter and shared joy replaced the mournful, repetitive attempts to reach God in a structured and forced way. That scene became part of family tradition. It reinforced the constant paternal reminder that we should have a healthy skepticism for those with power or position, even for those wearing the "cloth," and that we should be suspicious of those who believed there was only one way to achieve success, whatever that was. He wisely advised us "to beware of the people who genuflect too much," noting that the external trappings of religiosity rarely matched the necessary love and compassion promoted by Christ or Mohammed, Buddha or other spiritual leaders.

The subtle, steady, lasting forces of childhood noted above were captured by my father in the poetry of Latin and Greek masters as well as Irish bards, recited repeatedly at our kitchen table. Those early years of childhood and adolescence were a privileged period of protected discovery. We were happy and secure as part of a loving family. Particularly before the identity of each emerges, one's self seemed but an extension of an already existing organism.

Other organisms certainly flourished in our home. The oldest four children were boys, then came four girls. When we were young, we were told we would lose our essential oils if we took more than one hot bath a week. Even then we strongly suspected that the basis for this argument lay in the difficulty (and cost) of getting adequate hot water from the coal-fired heater. To make matters worse, all the boys had to use the same water; it was then changed for the girls. There must have been some deep and hidden Irish Catholic logic at play here.

When I was six, I firmly believed that the Nazis might well land on the beach at our summer home in New Jersey had not my brother John and I watched, carefully, from the upstairs window of a shingled house on a sand dune. We tried to identify the size and shape and sound of American planes so we could detect invaders, and looked for any strange new lights in the sky that might indicate danger. We could then shout to the Coast Guard warden protecting the shoreline on horseback–all before falling asleep at 8 p.m.

The interaction of God and State during the war was made very real to me, as a six year old who gave up jelly as his penance for Lent. That innocent gesture of sacrifice became inextricably linked and, importantly, allowed me to be involved with the American battle against the evil Japanese and Nazi empires. Having given up jelly I started to substitute butter on my morning bread. But, as my parents quickly noted, I was, in a period of butter rationing, really contributing to the fascist forces in the deadly global struggle, somehow being partially waged at our breakfast table by dietary restrictions. How confusing warfare was; I was soon ordered to resume my morning jelly.

In the Bronx I contributed to winning the war by dutifully collecting tin cans and newspapers that we were told would somehow be transformed into tanks, an evolution I never understood and would repeatedly question. I was also in charge of growing radishes in our backyard "Victory Garden." Radishes, I later learned, will grow anywhere and need almost no attention. But being young, and innocent, and very proud of the leafy blossoms above the soil and the bright red, hard bulbs beneath, I was glad to do my small part in the fight for freedom.

The author waiting for a baseball game to start, or maybe trying to decide how to handle a big bat, or dreaming of some other activity. It was then a much simpler era in the northeast Bronx: a large protective family, with an almost rural quality of neighbors with farm animals and unpaved streets.

Born Married

Very early–maybe at age five or six–my parents noted to me–and to anyone who wanted to listen–that I was somehow different from my siblings. This was explained–in the days when Irish Catholic immigrant families rarely thought of the possible psychological impact of tall tales–by my being told that I was the son of Mrs. Botchagalup, and I had been dropped off on our front stoop in a plain straw basket one cold winter day. Somehow this news didn't bother me, and I continued to thrive as part of an obviously slightly dysfunctional family group.

When I won a scholarship in the fifth grade, I declared that, henceforth, I would pay for my schooling and buy all my clothes, and I did. I was very young when my father once explained to my mother this stubborn streak, of being slightly apart from my brothers and sisters, by saying, "But, Gen, you know he was born married."

Our home was on a hill in a rural area of the Bronx near the New York/Mount Vernon border. The dirt roads were unpaved. It is almost inconceivable to recall, as I can so clearly, that patients in those years of the late 1930s and early 1940s paid my physician-father with home grown chickens, fresh eggs, and containers of goat's milk. "New York" (Manhattan) was like a distant land one heard about on the radio.

Growing up as a doctor's son–particularly since he was the first physician in a large, extended Irish immigrant family–allowed unusual experiences at a very early age. In that era tuberculosis was a terrible scourge, particularly for the poor living in crowded, often dirty tenements. Besides being a family doctor–a general practitioner–Dad had a special interest in tuberculosis and served as the Chest Consultant in several hospitals.

As a young boy I would accompany my father on house calls, sometimes being allowed to carry the wooden box that housed the pneumothorax machine. This apparatus of tubes and bubbling water fascinated me, especially as my father would explain its use–to partially collapse a portion of the lung as a therapy for tuberculosis abscesses. I can still see him performing this dangerous and painful procedure on obviously very sick patients in cold water flats; the patient would be carefully positioned leaning forward over the edge of a chair, and, without anesthesia, the tube would be inserted, the air let out slowly out of the chest cavity until the vacuum sealed the empty space.

Years later, remembering those fear-filled scenes, I asked my father what else a doctor could offer, in that pre-antibiotic era, to a consumptive, dying person. He answered, "You learned to listen, and sit on the side of the bed, and hold the patient's hand, and, sometimes, you would even give a hug." I've tried to use that approach many times, and, if I do it right, I can always recall those boyhood visits with my father to frightened patients whose faces I can still see.

There were other visits as a young doctor's helper that were equally memorable. The system of law in the northeast Bronx was, at that time and place, quite informal and very personal. If a friend or relative were picked up by the police for public drunkenness or domestic fights, the desk sergeant, almost always an Irish immigrant, would call the local doctor and ask that he come and take the violator home rather than "booking" him and thereby establishing a "record" that could endanger employment. Accompanying my father on these missions taught me to view the world–including close relatives–with slightly less deference, but with more compassion and understanding.

In our extended family of blood and "boat" relatives–the latter group having emigrated from the West of Ireland together–there was certainly too much alcohol imbibed. Maybe that adds to a child's memory of the period as a sensual, warm blur of Uncle Dan, Aunt Catherine, Uncle Jim's white socks, the Herliheys, the Kerry flats, Christmas Eve Mass, with the great benefit for our parents of not having to fast or abstain from midnight to morning services. They celebrated by having a cocktail at 11:45 p.m., and would then go straight to church, somehow believing they had "beat the system." Religion even influenced childhood sports; in our neighborhood the Catholics played against the Protestants in football and hockey. But there was ecumenical skiing in the neighborhood park, with the "big jump" being about four feet in Dr. Eden's Woods.

Our relatives seemed to be mostly policemen, and family friends were almost all of Irish extraction. There was enormous Dr. McDonald, probably weighing over 400 pounds, and his father; Pat, an Olympic weight thrower, who would allow us to run down his extended legs, the widths of a highway in a child's imagination, until we would wildly leap off into our father's arms. These gigantic figures seemed natural, for the Cahills were, we were told, descendants of the High Kings of Ireland. Even if the throne now apparently stood in Uncle Dinny's small apartment somewhere off Fordham Road in the Bronx, there was still a genetic nobility we accepted and treasured. After attending public school a short block from home, I was sent to Mt. St. Michael Academy from 5th through 12th grades. The teachers were Marist Brothers; my father once asked one of them, "why not go all the way?" Grade school years in the Bronx, are now recalled as a happy mélange of siblings, an inordinate number of relatives, and an endless cycle of holidays. There were Sunday dinners, usually late, meat always burnt, and interrupted by individual children's presentation of poetry or song, or dance on the sideboard, often with Dr. Collins (who delivered us all on the living room couch), and his family cheering us on.

Birthdays were very special in our home; a dinner menu one could choose, providing it didn't violate the scarcity imposed by war rationing; the birthday boy was excused from setting the table, clearing the dishes afterwards, and any washing or drying of the chipped crockery. Then came the singing of "Happy Birthday" that always ended with the line, "And he lived down in our alley." We knew we belonged to a tight-knit clan, even if there was only a metaphorical alley. After the cake came the presents, mostly, as I remember, thoughtfully selected, but often recycled books, sometimes with an earlier inscription to my father or mother. As my children and grandchildren know, I've kept that particular tradition very much alive. There were other, it often seemed constant, celebrations for reasons that ranged from graduations to becoming an altar boy, even to keeping the cellar medical office steps clear of ice and snow.

The office was an integral part of our family life. One was asked not to make too much noise when patients were there, and Dad would often bring the last patients upstairs for a drink. He would come up after office hours and put the cash of the day in the middle drawer in the dining room. It never entered anyone's mind that we would touch that drawer. After putting the money away he would read the notes we left for him on a hall table detailing our complaints or concerns and seek his intercession. Some notes found many years after his death concerned events such as "my brother hit me with a baseball bat." He would bring in the two boys and question the wisdom of trying to solve differences with violence, but then ask me why I had provoked such a strong reaction. It was an early lesson in conflict resolution. He said, "If it's important to you, write it down"; that early discipline stayed with me for life.

My high school memories are more of extracurricular involvements, from crosscountry, indoor and outdoor track, to editing the school newspaper and the yearbook, leading the Sodality with a lunchtime rosary in Lent broadcast over the loudspeakers so that all students had to participate whether they wanted to or not. Obviously, not everyone paid attention, and jokes and stories were inextricably mixed with prayers and blessings. First Friday Mass was rewarded with corn muffins at a deli/restaurant in Mt. Vernon. Except for Latin I cannot recall any stimulating lectures or teachers in high school. In fact, I was convinced by sophomore year that I knew as much (or more than) any of my teachers–quite a sad realization.

From the age of seven the small town of Point Lookout on Long Island was my magical refuge. I was unaware then that love lived just down the block. My wife Kate once gave me a childhood photo of herself picking a flower with a note stating, "You never knew the little girl in the garden but she must have known you were there–somewhere beyond the woods and flowers. And years later, when you found her, you never let her go; you loved and protected her through storms and sunrises. But most of all, you let the little girl survive and continue to bloom and grow–in her own way."

I saw my first death one early morning in Point Lookout at age eight when a neighbor's wife came yelling at our door for help. Her husband had had a heart attack, and carrying my father's medical bag I watched as a man gasping for air with obvious chest pain, quickly died. He was Sidney Hillman, the head of the Women's Garment Union and the person President Roosevelt designated to select his 1944 Vice President. When FDR said "clear it with Sidney" to assure labor backing, he chose Harry Truman. Shortly after his death, President Truman called Mrs. Hillman on the phone while I stood in silent awe as a child in the room. Years later Mrs. Hillman and her daughter became patients of mine, closing an historical loop in my life.

Point Lookout is the town where my roots are deepest and where Kate's ashes are awaiting mine. There were close childhood and adolescent "crowds" of friends–influencing my social development, allowing me to learn how to share and cooperate. As teenagers in that innocent era we would hitchhike after school recessed on Friday from the Bronx to Point Lookout.

Kate as a young girl; her elegance and sensitivity are captured in this photo. She once wrote that even before we met she somehow knew I was nearby and that I would encourage, and assure, in every way, her own search for beauty. We shared a great love for many decades.

Overcoming Barriers

Jobs were an essential part of our growing up. From age six or seven, on alternate weeks at home, one was assigned to clearing the table, washing or drying dishes, hanging dozens of diapers with wooden clothespins, shoveling the winter snow. My father captured my attitude of life by observing, when I was eight years of age: "If you ask Kevin nicely, he will shovel all day; if you ask him rudely he'll throw the shovel at you and walk away."

In Point Lookout I delivered newspapers from Tom Dier's tiny, dirty house on Lido Boulevard. With the same perverse joy I experienced at the time, I well recall a later job as a hamburger/hot dog chef for a rich Greek beach concessionaire at the local Town Park. He would buy fresh sirloin steak for his spoiled son, only to have us employees switch, at the last minute, his costly delicacy with the rotten meat, highly peppered to disguise its smell, that he was serving to the public. With a brother and two friends we once formed a twelve year old's company and created our own business card: "we'll wash your bathrooms, clean your windows and clear your empty lots." The group was so memorable that, many years later, when I tried to bargain with the owner over the price asked for our present summer house, she said, "Buy it, Kevin. You liked the house when you cleaned the toilets." So I did.

I undoubtedly met Kate before our teen age years since her brother Frank was a childhood friend. But memory dates my vivid recognition of her to age 14, when, possibly hormonal, or with greater awareness of beauty and intelligence,

I became fascinated with her sensitivity, elegance, ease and knowledge. Many years later, at a memorial service after she died, a friend wrote, "They met at 14 and fell into a passionate love from which neither ever recovered."

That summer I was a Good Humor Boy–biking ice cream around town with a set of bells on the handlebar to attract customers.When the delivery truck would bring the daily supplies–to be kept cold by dry ice in the box at the front of the bike–one received credit for five broken popsicles per box of 100. Every day the first stop on my tour of town was Kate's house. I would offer a free ice cream "on a stick"–toasted almond was her favorite. It was a teenager's way of expressing something special–affection, respect, maybe desire. One way or the other, it worked, and we would talk for a while, and then my day seemed perfect.

I felt I could do anything once she smiled at–or for–me; that reaction lasted all my life. Many times, as the years unfolded, she would say, "Kevin, you just didn't get enough cookies when you were a child"–her way of explaining how a kind and gentle act always motivated me far more than a cold order or demand. When I became testy at inconsequential events–or people–she would call me aside and gently say, "I love you." I would then work happily for another few months till the cycle would need to be renewed.

Weekends and summers in Point Lookout were idyllic. It is a small town, only 11 by 3 blocks, bounded by water–the ocean, an inlet, and the bay–on three sides, and protected on the fourth by five miles of public park. The town allows no car parking and has a 15 mph speed limit. It was (and remains) a children's paradise. Friendships were formed, social patterns and group interactions evolved, in an innocent setting where gatherings rotated from home to home almost every night among the "crowd" of 15 boys and 15 girls. Until 16 years of age I had to be home ahead of the 10 p.m. curfew enforced by my father, watching the world carefully from his bench on our front steps.

At the end of that summer I was lucky to find a job as a beach club pool lifeguard; for the next six summers I was an ocean lifeguard. This was a great way to see the world, from an elevated perch, in the sun and wind, with daily swims and occasional dramatic rescues. We spent an inordinate amount of time lathering ourselves with baby oil and iodine to realize the deepest tan, and years later, skin cancer. There was the great seaweed strike; clam and beer parties; finding bags of U.S. mail (discarded by a very lazy postal carrier) floating in the surf on a foggy day in Lido.

The reason my lifeguard career flourished was quite simple. In that era most lifeguards were "career men;" they would travel to Florida in the winter and come back to Long Island in the summer. What they possessed in muscle power was rarely matched in the intellectual sphere.

I entered the lifeguard hierarchy as a 5 foot 6 inch, 140 pound swimmer who was unreasonably certain that I could accomplish with understanding and skill what my colleagues obviously could do based solely on their sheer size and strength. I recall how proud I was of that first lifeguard bathing suit, the silver whistle, and the incredible joy of pulling a drowning child from the surf. But reality soon intruded on our uncomplicated beach life.

On a hot July 4th, a strike was called over the very important issue of whether lifeguards had to rake seaweed from the beachfront. The lifeguards felt it embarrassing, particularly in front of their girlfriends, to undertake such a lowly job, and they went to the picket line in 95 degree temperature on a crowded Independence Day at the Town Park. The elderly, staid Commissioner tried to reason with the senior lifeguards but was greeted with a string of four letter words, a fairly common means of their locker room communication. The Commissioner promptly ejected the lifeguard leaders and vowed that the strike would continue all summer, "through Labor Day if need be."

Maybe the impending idea of a summer off the lifeguard stands made the leaders desperate enough to turn to their youngest, shortest, but possibly most talkative, new colleague. I was asked to intervene and try to convince the Commissioner that they meant no harm by their earthy expressions, and that their cause was just. After a few hours, the Commissioner agreed with my logic, but insisted that, henceforth he would only deal with me.

I was appointed Chief Lifeguard. Summers became a wondrous time, with daily swimming and the added, almost unique, experience of being administrator of eighty-five decent, but trouble-prone, muscle men. I came to understand the dreams and desires of a group utterly different from those I had known, and I learned how to forge a team from very diverse elements. Why they became members of that team was sometimes based on very personal factors.

I hired one lifeguard because he had a Jaguar with a roll back roof for the driver; he became my chauffeur as I checked ten miles of ocean beaches. Another, Frank Keefe, was lured to be my assistant after he leapt from the floor of a bar in Atlantic Beach one afternoon and, finishing with a perfect pirouette, declared that he was a flower rising before St. Francis. He became a character in our lives; many years later he composed a ballet, Brendan the Navigator, to celebrate the birth of our fourth son.

Point Lookout had a peculiar attraction for Mafia mob figures; maybe it was the isolation, or the fact that the Irish and Italian first generation formed, by and large, a non-judgmental community. One could always identify Mafia houses by the chains, or ornate gates, across a driveway, by the white brick they favored, and, often enough, by tall men in three-piece suits who (from across the street) watched the inhabitant's movements through binoculars. People in suits in a summer beach town stand out, and we, as young teenagers, would be bold and ask them, "Are you FBI?" Whatever they said, we knew the answer.

Francis Ford Coppola, who later produced and directed *The Godfather* movies, lived in town. Point Lookout landmarks featured prominently in *The Godfather*, with Sonny being killed at the toll booth entrance to our town, and the Corleone family compound a replica of a Mafia domain in the small neighboring hamlet of Lido.

A heavily guarded house there was owned by a mobster popularly known as "Three Fingers Brown." As a young lifeguard I proposed that we could run Children's Day Races, and have a party, all at no cost, if some of the wealthy citizens would provide refreshments and prizes. "Three Fingers" clearly had the biggest house in town, a modern day fortress.

In my lifeguard bathing suit, and nothing else lest the thugs standing around the driveway misinterpret the purpose of my visit, I walked boldly to his front door, knocked and the owner appeared: "We would like you to donate CocaCola for Children's Day, Mr. Brown." "My name's Lucchese," he responded. I thought he was trying to get out of donating and I persisted: "Everyone knows you're Three Fingers Brown" and he, quite angry, repeated, "My name's Lucchese." As I saw his bodyguards start moving toward me I realized it was the wrong argument in the wrong place. Someone less threatening provided the CocaCola and a good time was had by all. Those who took our swimming lessons won all the prizes, favored by shifting tides, and a moving finish line in the surf controlled by the lifeguards.

One final benefit of the lifeguard job was to lead to my first teaching position. The Post Office, in gratitude for retrieving a mail bag that had been thrown in the ocean by a disgruntled worker, gave me a Christmas season job unloading bags at a Bronx depot. The bags were heavy and the career workers were very well built, and clearly didn't see me "pulling my weight." After some discussion, I offered to give a lecture on any topic of their choosing every night during their 2am lunch break. We would agree on a topic the previous night, and I would research an encyclopedia providing a 45 minute talk; the talks seemed to please my captive audience. One was on "atoms," another on "colors," another on "stars." I was then told to rest on the mail bags till dawn, and go back to my studies, a luxury they knew would not be granted to them.

By age 16 I realized, in an overwhelming way that persisted until she died, that I loved Kate. We would sit on the rocks on the Lynbrook Avenue jetty and she would, at first, allow only her head to rest on my shoulder. Any embrace was measured–by me, out of respect, maybe out of fear. By the end of the next summer, however, she said I could rub her back. I thought I had gone to heaven. In troubled times, even many decades later, I would lie by her side, rub her back, and somehow knew it would all be okay as long as we were together.

Tying Knots

Reality, inevitably, intruded. High school had blessedly ended. When I discussed college options with my father he succinctly summarized my choices, "wherever the nickel takes you"–the price of a subway ride. It also went without saying that it should be a Catholic college. The nickel defined one's alma mater. I had received a scholarship to Fordham University in the Bronx, and from the day I arrived on their lovely Rose Hill campus, the intellectual challenges, and the joy of exploration and learning, were almost palpable. Majoring in the classics and philosophy, both strong Jesuit fields of study, and being part of the Honors Club, allowed one to walk in an academic gown among the ivy colored halls, as well as under that ultimate touch of reality, the nearby elevated trains, or through the quiet beauty of the Bronx Botanical Gardens, and debate the insoluble questions of youth. Were Hellenic and Helladic the same?

Being poor, and trying to be an entrepreneur (although, as life later proved, with almost no material sense), I felt the Fordham mascot, a ram, could, and almost morally should, be incorporated and then sold, in small shares, at local women's colleges. With a few friends we bought a rather rundown ram from a derelict farm in New Jersey, printed colorful stocks, and quickly sold 100 at $10 per share, far more than the value of the beast, or his supplies. To the dismay of my more conservative classmates, I felt the world–or at least the women's colleges–needed, or at least would buy, even more shares in the ram. I bought out the hesitant, and printed and sold over a hundred additional stock shares. It was my only successful "public offering"; we had great fun.

With minimal college science courses, I was accepted into Harvard Medical School after three years as part of an experiment to determine "did pre-med matter?". My father urged me not to accept the scholarship, arguing that one's final year in College was almost a last chance to unabashedly immerse oneself in ancient culture and modern art before starting on a lifelong professional journey. That year I played water polo at the NYAC; I went to museums and theaters. My father died later that year, and this grateful son never forgot his wisdom or his perspective on life.

In the traditions of Irish immigrants, the wake for my father was in our home in the Bronx, with a keg of beer in the backyard, priests saying endless rosaries, and patients and relatives mourning, with tears, even "keening" the ancient Irish wailing. Somehow food came out of the kitchen and dishes seemed to be miraculously recycled. I was told by an old aunt that Kate was running the kitchen, and so she was. And so she did until she died. There was no looking back from that day forth.

After Kate died I found letters indicating that we almost, quite madly, planned to marry earlier that year. I had won a grant to go to London for a summer program and this would pay for our honeymoon. The trip never materialized because my father was dying–which he did that September. But emotionally, from that time on, I was married.

I entered Cornell Medical School the day my father died. The next four years were an incredibly fulfilling experience, a gradual realization of a way of life, one that became an essential part of my being. There was an intellectual excitement in mastering the complexities of anatomy and pathology, of learning how to diagnose illnesses and care for patients. They were certainly not an easy four years. Since my brothers were away much of the time, I tried to visit my mother and four young sisters as often as possible. My mother's situation was quite sad: she had become the receptionist in my father's medical office where the physician was now her brother. He humiliated her in small, petty ways that took a toll on her spirit, and there was little anyone could do to help her. Her deepest desire was, I always felt, to die and join her "Pete" in heaven.

Although I had a medical school scholarship for tuition I had absolutely no extra money for room, board or books. I worked as a chemistry lab technician several nights a week from 9 p.m. to 6 a.m., and then went to class from 9 a.m. to 5 p.m. I would sleep on the floor under the chemistry machine grateful for the few hours of rest. I would also translate medical articles, from almost any language. I wonder now how I managed, but youth, determination and Kate's support were the necessary ingredients for survival. There was almost no outside social life, setting a pattern we followed, not unhappily, in the years ahead. We found joy and great satisfaction in museums, music, books, and each other. I met a few great teachers who encouraged critical thinking, and exposed a novice to the wisdom of masters.

Dr. Harry Gold was my main mentor; a renowned cardiologist and pharmacologist, he had devised the "double blind" study to eliminate the bias of physicians as well as patients in clinical drug trials. He never received the honor he deserved, that of Chairman of the Department, because he was Jewish, and there was overt prejudice in those years. A sad example of the elitist, WASP atmosphere that dominated the Cornell/

New York Hospital in the 1950s was the response from the Dean, slightly inebriated at a class Christmas party, to a question from this freshman student: "Is there prejudice in the admission policy?" He blithely replied, "Hell no, we take five Catholics and five Jews a year, and a nigger every five years."

Dr. Gold taught me why, and how, to challenge accepted dogma, to always search for new explanations and solutions. He also sponsored my first steps in a career in tropical medicine by securing a Lehman Fellowship during the last semester of my third medical school year. The "Lehman" connection was my pulmonary teacher, Dr. Edgar Mayer, who figured prominently in my later professional life in New York as a generous and wise counselor. For 28 years he was in a tuberculosis sanatorium in upper New York State, and taught me how to be patient, and careful in dealing with complex illnesses. He practiced the Hippocratic Oath which urges, *primum non nocere*–the first thing in making medical decisions is "to do no harm."

I traveled around the world, first through the Middle East and then on a two month journey in a 3rd class railroad car, through poverty stricken India, from the slums of Bombay to the peaceful marshes of Kerala, to Madras where I thought I would die of amebic dysentery, to recovery at the Christian Medical College in Vellore, through Hyderabad to Delhi, and a week with Prime Minister Jawaral Nehru. Dr. Mayer had cared for the Prime Minister's tubercular sister, Mrs. Krishna Hutheesingh. Nehru invited me to stay with him in Government House; we talked about plants, played bridge and established a bond that served me well throughout many future medical trips to India. I later treated both his daughter and grandson (both Prime Ministers). As in family practice, the most important ties in my medical life have been based on word-of-mouth recommendations, and the trust and confidence that come from caring for individual sick patients.

After meandering through the outposts of Rajasthan, and seeing the moon rise over the fort in Jaisalmer, I was ready to begin my work in Calcutta. There I lived above an orphanage in Howrah, walking daily across the Hooghly River to work as an intern at the All India Institute of Tropical Medicine. Being young and indefatigable, I would then spend hot afternoons helping an unknown Albanian nun in her nearby gutter hospice for the dying. Years later she became famous as Mother Theresa; we stayed in close touch until she died.

My own introduction to tropical medicine, and to the interrelationships of poverty and disease, occurred in India as I fell in love with a way of life. I found romance in the settings that others might see only as dirty, broken-down wastelands. Surely those negatives existed in Calcutta. But amidst the fetid stenches of Indian urban decay, I could close my eyes and see saffron robes rather than soiled rags. I could hear music in the cacophonous sounds of the slums, and in the long silence of a city drenched in the humid heat that comes with monsoon rains. Yet, with patience, and respect for others' human dignity, by balancing passion and compassion, by practicing civility and trying to understand the bases for hostility in those we assist, one can learn many lessons–particularly from the dispossessed and oppressed, and develop a special approach to life.

In the midst of such harsh reality, one can also find great beauty. My wife used to say that I was the only person she knew who could come home after three months in a refugee camp and keep her awake all night describing, in great detail, how lovely so many parts of the experience were. Obviously, there were incredible scenes of sadness and evil, but there were also exquisite sunrises and sunsets in the desert, and the magical sounds of children laughing, and the incredible strength of mothers and grandmothers coping in a daily struggle to survive. Much depends on how the mind's eye sees, and interprets, the field in which we labor.

Having survived several months in the dirt and stifling heat of a Calcutta summer, I journeyed–by a narrow track railroad car–through the Bengal tea country to the hill station of Darjeeling. There, determined to learn how to climb in the high Himalayas, I applied to the Mountaineering Institute founded by Sir Edmund Hillary, the first westerner to reach the top of Mt. Everest. However, an insurmountable obstacle prevented my enrollment–a hefty tuition fee. Quickly adapting to reality, I walked across town and knocked on the door of the Sherpa Climbers' Association.

When I told the Sherpa secretary that I wanted to join their organization, a crowd of dirty, muscular peasants came out and, with pointing fingers and derisive gestures, they laughed at me. But I had a persuasive argument and convinced them that if they let me climb with them I would provide basic medical care for their families. Besides, I noted, "I'm short and squat just like you, and strong enough to carry my own load."

I spent almost six weeks climbing with them, learning the mysteries and wonder of the mountains through the eyes and spirit of the Sherpas. We went to over 19,000 feet one day, with packs and no oxygen. In my office, hidden behind a tall light are two treasured items. One is my member's insignia in the Sherpa Association–I was the only Caucasian member then and, for all I know, may still retain that special honor. It was won by hard work and sharing. The other memento is a traditional sherpa knife, a kukri, inscribed on its crude black leather case: "To Shri Kevin Cahill from Tenzing Norkay, India, 1959"–a deeply appreciated gift from another world, but one reflecting that it is possible to cross the most traditional cultural barriers if you are willing to "carry your own load" and contribute in some way. Gratitude for medical care was to open many doors in the years ahead.

That summer there was a constant stream of refugees in Darjeeling, including the Dalai Lama and his entourage fleeing Tibet, carting whole temples on their heads and shoulders. Equally bizarre was a game of bridge at the Darjeeling Club where a Canadian journalist and I beat the opposing couple, a lovely young American girl named Hope Cooke who had just met a wizened, impressive man. Judging from the number of servants, he was someone very important in those high mountain lands. By the end of the bridge game we learned he was the visiting ruler from a neighboring kingdom. The defeated pair went off for a walk and, fairly soon after, they were married in a fantasy wedding, she becoming the American Queen of Sikkim.

I returned to my base in Calcutta, bade farewell to friends at the Tropical Institute, to the orphans I had come to love, to the dying and those who cared for them, as well as to the poets and artists I had discovered. Where one, overwhelmed at first, thinks there is only misery I had discovered joy. I then set off on the final stage of a medical sojourn through the

After completing a semester in Calcutta, I traveled to the Himalayas to experience the challenges of high mountain climbing. Since a tuition fee for Westerners prevented my attending the best known school in the area, I joined the Sherpa Climbers' Association, and shared their duties, learning the significance of carrying my own equipment. At the end of a memorable stay, Tenzing Norkay, the first Sherpa to reach the peak of Mount Everest, presented a kukri to his new partner.

SHERPA-CLIMBERS'-ASSOCIATION

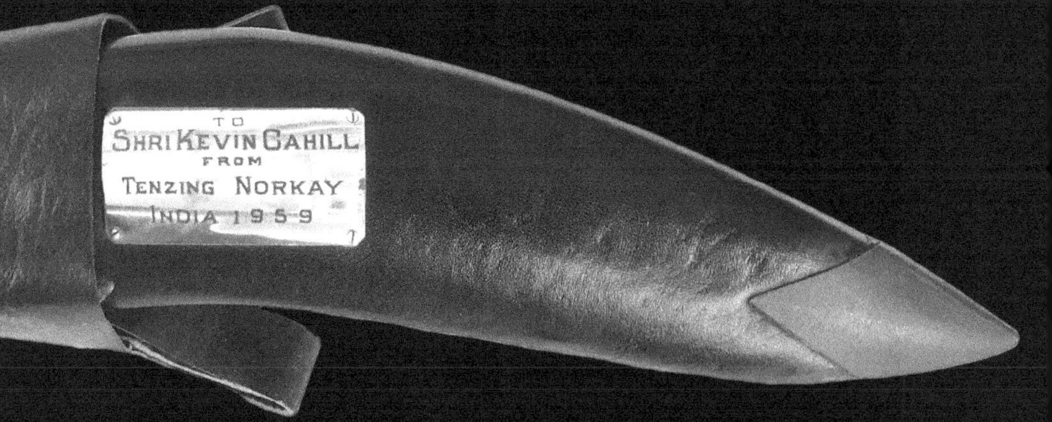
TO
SHRI KEVIN CAHILL
FROM
TENZING NORKAY
INDIA 1959

Dr. Edgar Mayer, one of America's leading pulmonary physicians, was my teacher and mentor. He provided the funds for my first medical grant as a Lehman Traveling Fellow, allowing me to spend months at the Tropical Disease Institute in Calcutta, India, and to slowly traverse Asia before the decades of war closed many parts to any travel. When I was discharged from the Navy he gave me a rent-free room in his Fifth Avenue office providing that I would devote half of my time to academic work–an incredible gift to a young physician. The office has been my New York base for over 50 years.

ATIONAL

Far East, first to the Viet Nam hill country, just before the war engulfed the area.

As one example of that impending disaster fear was almost palpable in the air; when I went to Cambodia I was the only passenger on the plane to Siem Reap where I wanted to spend a day at the temple of Angkor Wat. There was no hotel open in the town. I went to a tea shop where, fortuitously, I met a Frenchman who kindly invited me to stay in his empty home, his colleagues and family having fled. He was Philip Grosslier, the archeologist who wrote the classic text *The Art and Architecture of Angkor.* Instead of a brief stop, I spent ten magical days exploring one of the world's wonders with the man who had studied the site for thirty years. Cambodia shortly became a no-man's land under American bombardment and, later, the Khmer Rouge. Timing is everything in life.

In India, and throughout rural Asia, I had seen death and disease on a vast scale. I had also come to appreciate how ignorant I was of so many ancient cultures, incredibly rich in music, drama, painting, philosophy and spirituality. I returned completely and forever changed. I recall an early welcome home dinner in Point Lookout when I tried to explain, to a very puzzled family, that Hindus believed they might come back in the afterlife as a cow or an insect. This, I told them, was why they treated cattle as sacred and why they wore masks–in case one inhaled a parent or grandparent. I was not certain where I stood on this profound spiritual question; the dinner was a disaster.

One of the most important lessons of India that has remained with me for life, and helped determine what I have tried to do and how, was the realization that one must stay calm and focused in the midst of chaos if one wanted to help others. There was no time in such situations for self-indulgent, personal cares or concerns. The petty needs that so often dominate our lives distract us from getting critical tasks accomplished. Whatever the fears, I realized they simply didn't matter much in the face of what others were suffering every day, all day, in the disaster that life offered them.

Kate spent these six months on her own journey of discovery, traveling westward to Japan, and then on through the Middle East and Europe. After circumnavigating the globe in opposite directions, we arrived home at the same time, met in Point Lookout, and realized that, whatever lay ahead, we probably wouldn't travel alone again. Henceforth, we would face the world as one. Kate said that while she didn't know if we could make a marriage work, she knew she couldn't live without me. I never had any doubts we were meant to be together and, slowly but surely, we became intertwined forever.

Examining a Sudanese patient with visceral leishmaniasis (kala-azar) in the mid 1960's. This highly fatal, parasitic infection invades the organs and bone marrow. One can visualize a swollen spleen in the patient. My base in South Sudan was in Malakal Upper Nile Province, hundreds of miles south of Khartoum. At the time it was a conflict zone with Dinka, Shilluk & Nuer tribes fighting each other and the Arabs from the north. Sad to say it is currently (60 years later) once again the epicenter of famine, rape and murder in South Sudan.

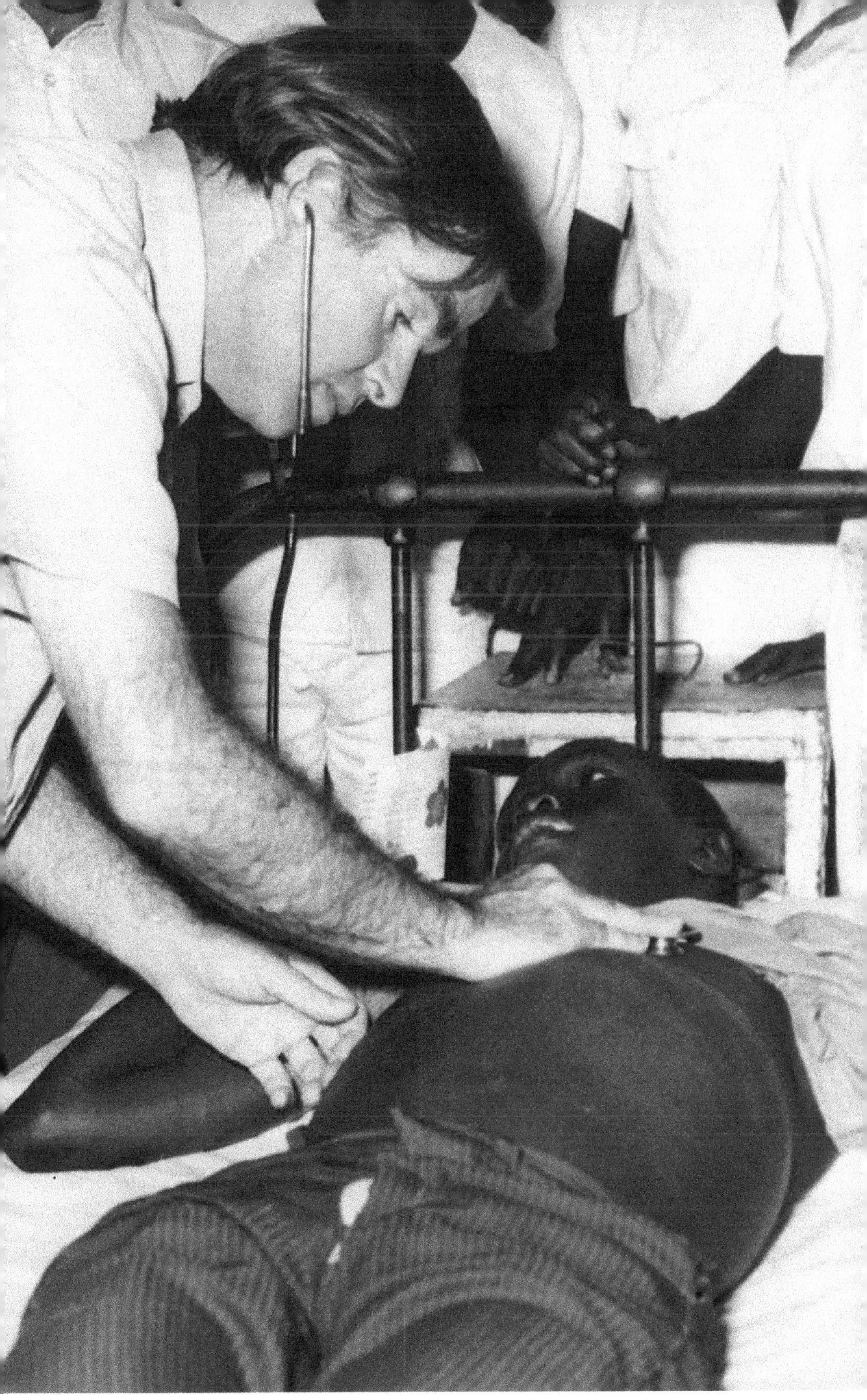

Severe malnutrition in Somalia with the classic picture of marasmus–swollen belly, stick like limbs, and the vacant stare of a hungry, dying, child.

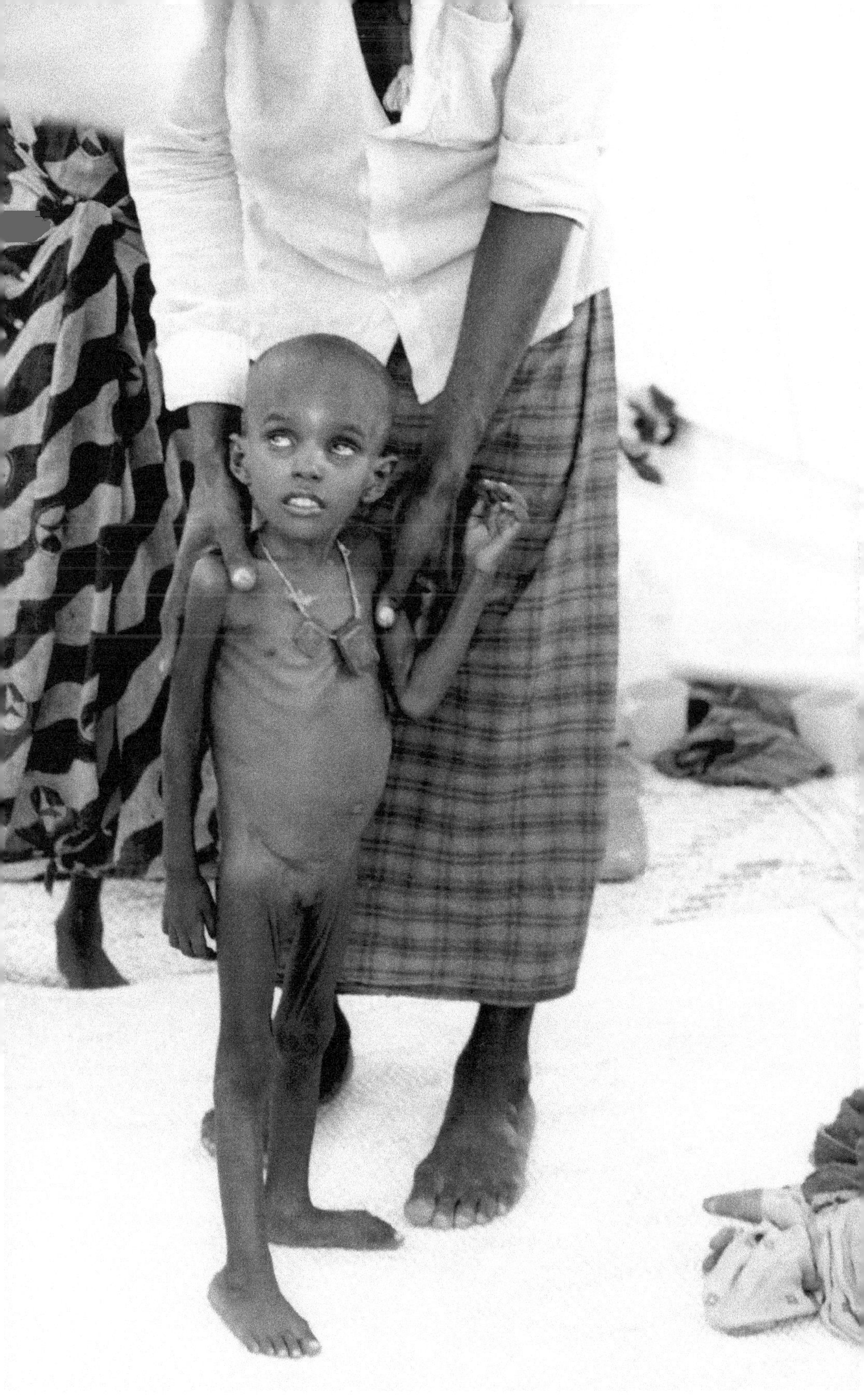

Intertwined

I had been appointed as a substitute intern at Bellevue Hospital in New York City, and there, in its Catholic chapel, we soon formalized our long delayed engagement. As I began a monologue–possibly practiced for years–expressing my love, and asking for her hand in sacred matrimony, a drunken man sleeping in a pew at the back of the church awakened from his stupor saying: "For God's sake, can't a man find quiet anywhere?" We walked over to the solitude of the Jewish chapel and, in its Talmudic silence, I offered Kate my humble betrothal ring.

Within a few days I left for England on a Fellowship in liver diseases under a great teacher, Professor Sheila Sherlock. This pattern of sudden departures, and periods of long separation, was part of the life we knew would face us in international health and tropical medicine. We missed many of the usual events that characterized the prenuptial period. But we never really felt the loss of, as Kate phrased it, "fake, false wedding showers." Loneliness was, nonetheless, very real, and when Kate died I found a box with my daily letters from that period full of plans for our future, and of an utterly unjustified belief that she would enjoy hearing all the details of how one did liver biopsies or drained ascitic fluid from the abdomen of a cirrhotic patient.

When Professor Sherlock learned we were planning to meet in Ireland at Christmas she asked if I could give a lecture and thereby get a free air ticket from London to Dublin. The answer was obvious. We quickly decided on a topic, and, using her contacts with colleagues, who later became my friends,

I headed off to Ireland. One of the problems with this maiden public lecture on "Hepatitis in Pregnancy" at the ancient Jervis Street Hospital was its timing: 4 p.m. on December 24th. Half way through my undoubtedly overly serious talk, a somewhat inebriated physician muttered loudly, "Ah, Mister, will you sit down, it's Christmas Eve." Even if the audience may have long forgotten the hepatologic details I presented, I certainly remember that introduction to The Royal College of Surgeons in Ireland, an institution that became part of our lives for many decades ahead. I also learned a very important lesson on appropriate timing in academia.

Later that night I traveled across a sodden, silent Ireland to meet my bride-to-be. Our families had to be consulted about this premarital journey; their approval was duly sought, and we finally ended up, much in love, being alone with one another in Shannon. The drive down to Kerry took us through Limerick City which had a banner across their main street proudly declaring that we were in "The home of the largest Sodality to the Blessed Virgin." It all seemed, at least to me, like a plot to prevent us from consummating our love in some remote hotel.

So we drove on, arriving late at night at the Cahill family farm in the small village of Rathmore. Even here fates intervened, and my dreams remained dreams. An ancient Aunt, Catherine, sat in a chair, all night, in the hallway between Kate's bedroom and mine. Love may be passionate, and desires strong, but in those years they were only to be shared in certain ways until marriage. Nonetheless, we had a wonderful time together, with country dances, long poems appreciated by the number of stanzas one could recite from memory, learning Kerry myths, and coming to appreciate the peculiar atonal, nasal songs that gave joy until dawn. We later translated these rich memories into our own family life, making long car rides more tolerable by teaching the children to sing and recite those same songs and stories, using the rural Kerry accent. They became very accomplished mimics, and old traditions were preserved and passed on to a new generation.

A few months later we finally arranged to be married in a ten day open period after I was to return from England and before I was to begin a rotation that required living in a hospital. The secretary for Kate's parish had accepted her reservation for a Nuptial Mass at 10:00 a.m. on a Saturday morning. Kate's parents had reserved their Golf Club for the reception and invitations were printed and sent out. One month before the wedding the pastor called Kate saying it was all an error, and that church weddings with a formal Mass were not allowed during Lent. That was the rule and there would be no exception.

Kate called me in London in a panic. I boldly telephoned Francis Cardinal Spellman (who knew my long deceased father) and explained the problem, arguing that we should not be penalized for the Church's error, and that, furthermore, the rule shouldn't be applied so rigidly to those who had no control over their medical schedules. That surely could not be God's intent. He agreed, called the pastor, and Kate was told by that very proper man that "he can order me to give you the church but he can't order me to perform the wedding service." A number of telephone calls later from London (no simple task for this destitute fiancé) Father Fagan, the liberal, Irish-born pastor in Point Lookout, agreed to marry us, and he did so in a beautiful ceremony on a clear cold March day.

At the end of the Nuptial Mass he read from a parchment, in a loud voice, a very Special Papal Blessing issued by the Holy Father for "this young couple." When I asked him after Mass if we could have the Blessing for our wedding scrapbook, he explained that there wasn't one; it had been merely a way he wished to "rub the nose" of the cranky pastor who was unhappily watching the scandalous ceremony from the back of the church.

On the night before the wedding I had stayed at one of Kate's sibling's house. My brother John, our best man, came in the morning, helped me dress in formal tails, and we went off in his old car for the church. The car broke down on the Southern State Parkway; I had to get out and, in all my finery, push the car until we were rescued by a sympathetic, and highly amused, man who drove us to the church. That wasn't the end of our wedding escapades.

After a lovely reception, with dancing and tossing the bridal garter, we embarked on married life looking fresh and confident, but really quite confused. We had borrowed an old Volkswagen and were going to "honeymoon" in restored Colonial Williamsburg, Virginia. Our first night was to be in a New York hotel. I went to the reservation desk and asked for a "double bed." When the clerk started to laugh, I became quite insistent, saying we were legally married and I wanted a double bed (instead of a double room). The manager came, smiled on us, and ordered a suite, sent up champagne, and we thought the world was wonderful.

The second night we arrived in Washington, D.C. I called my brother Michael, a Georgetown medical student who knew the city well, and told him we were on the outskirts in a somewhat rundown place called "The White House." He informed us it was best known as a low class whorehouse; so much for my good taste and planning. Finally, on day 3, we arrived in Williamsburg, but quickly discovered we didn't have enough money for a hotel room. Sadly, we drove through town until we found a cheap motel. Everything was fine from then on.

Kate and I lived for the next few months in one room with an electric frying pan as our only kitchen utensil. When we once ran almost completely out of money, I found a sign on a telephone pole advertising a shipment of cases of sardines for some ridiculously low cost. We ate sardines for almost a month, cooked in the most imaginative ways. Neither of us ever ate a sardine again.

I had graduated from medical school utterly broke (I recall the largest gift was a five dollar bill from my mother) but we somehow lived, quite nicely, on my $50/month salary as an intern and Kate's $65/week salary as an assistant to an interior decorator. We found a studio apartment on the corner of Christopher and Bleecker in Greenwich Village. If there were a cheese shop opening in the Village we would be there, knowing they might offer free samples.

Once, while working in the Emergency Department at St. Vincent's Hospital, I cared for a man who had been burned with hot coffee while dining at "The Steak Joint." The grateful owner told me to come for a free dinner with Kate, by now very large with child. We went out the next Saturday evening, gorging ourselves on a good steak and dessert. The problem was that we were in "The Steak Place," a neighboring restaurant. When the bill came I explained the promise of the owner, but quickly discovered it was the wrong restaurant.

I had to tell the proprietor that I had no money; he laughed and asked if I'd give as good care to the next patron of his establishment who became ill and ended up at St. Vincent's. We escaped, well fed, poor, happy, and in love, into the Greenwich Village night, with our own tales and stories.

During that intern year I wrote articles in leading medical journals including *The Lancet,* the *New England* and the *New York Journals of Medicine*, and an editorial in the *Annals of Internal Medicine* (something one usually does after decades of professional life). One of the articles, to give an example of the drive that sustained us, was on an interesting patient who had been hospitalized with jaundice. He was a janitor, and for some reason I cannot recall, I considered leptospirosis in my differential diagnosis. This is a rare (in New York City) illness transmitted by spirochetal organisms in the urine of rats. It seemed quite natural–at least to me–that we, my very pregnant wife and I, should go to his building, see if we could catch some rats, and determine if indeed the infecting organisms were present. So with traps provided by the patient, we laid out our bait, caught the rats, proved the presence of the *Leptospira ictohemorragia*, and wrote an article for a leading medical journal.

As I was finishing my internship year, the uncle who had taken over my father's medical office said to me, "Come, turn the key in the door and you can make $100,000 a year." I didn't want that life, especially with that uncle, and told Kate I was determined to pursue a career in tropical medicine. She said, "Do whatever you feel is best, and I will always be with you." For the rest of my professional life I was able to do what I did–what we did–because of that shared commitment.

I had been awarded a National Institute of Health (NIH) grant to pursue training in tropical medicine in London. Shortly before departure, however, I was informed that the Fellowship was, because of a national budgetary crisis, "approved but not funded," a phrasing I never forgot. Not quite sure what to do, I once again called Francis Cardinal Spellman and explained my plight. At a brief interview in his Residence, I suggested that he must know foundations that could replenish the cancelled $7,500 grant. Unfortunately, he said, the sum was "too small" for him to go to a foundation. He abruptly left the room only to return a few minutes later with a check for the amount and said, "You owe me nothing; go and do what you have said you want to do in tropical medicine." Within the month, the NIH restored the grant. I was able to return the Cardinal's check, but never, ever, forgot his confidence and generosity.

The memories of the early years of our marriage are extremely vivid–maybe even more than my recollections of recent events. I can describe every one of the furnishings in our first one room apartment, especially the creative decorating changes that became necessary when our son Kevin was born. His crib was ceremoniously placed in the bathroom.

As was true of all young American doctors at the time, I had been drafted into the military (U.S. Navy in my instance). Fortunately, they allowed me to return to London to continue my research, and complete a Diploma in Tropical Medicine at the University of London, and the London School of Hygiene and Tropical Medicine. In London we lived in the top two floors of an old Georgian house overlooking Hampstead Heath. Maybe–if I really try–I can recall some cold nights where extra heat had to be produced from an electric bar, fed by pennies, that worked for five or ten minutes. Mostly I recall the warmth of love under a puffy duvet. In any event the heater was only for young Kevin's room, which, again, was located in a large bathroom. Kate once heard an English visitor say to his wife, "My God, they probably flush the loo to serenade the baby to sleep." We may well have.

One of the perks of being a young Lieutenant in the Navy Medical Corps in London was that we could dine in class, and at minimal cost, at the American Officers' Club. We certainly became very skilled in finding free concerts all over London. That year England also allowed us to travel through Wales and Scotland in our bright red VW; to go to the opera at Covent Garden for ten shillings; to spend Christmas holidays back on the family farm in rural Kerry, there dancing in barns with sheep tethered to bare walls, while songs and stories went on long after the bar closed. We had not stayed at the family home before as a properly married couple, and were now given the grand bedroom above the bar–Aunt Catherine would not have allowed that intimacy on our last visit.

Kate put young Kevin in bed, closed the window to divert the moist Kerry air from her baby. Suddenly smoke filled the room; Kate had no way of knowing that the pathway for the bar smoke was directed, circuitously, through the bedroom and out the open window, for the chimney above had been blocked for years. Kate called for help, and all the local farmers came up to see what these innocent Americans had done to a system that had worked so well for generations.

She decided to try to get some sleep while I returned downstairs to buy rounds of "pints" for the town. When I came up Kate said that a slat was loose in the bed and I tried to reposition it. The bed collapsed, causing great amazement from the crowd below, and they again trooped up to admire "the wonder of it all." For years after, as we took inexpensive holidays in Kerry from our base in the Middle East, the locals would say, "Ah, he's a small fellow, but do you remember the night he collapsed the bed."

Another experience that characterized, for us, rural Ireland at that time occurred when we stopped our car near a roadside pump so that we could change young Kevin's soiled diaper. As Kate was putting a clean "nappy" on, I was pumping out water to wash the dirty one. I saw an old farmer striding across the muddy field towards me and, being an urban American, thought he would say something critical about using his pump without permission. But he silently bent down, cut a cabbage from its stalk, and offered it to me. Surprised, I said I didn't really want a cabbage; he cut another, and again offered it to me saying, "Mister if I'm here next year I'll plant more, and if I'm not I don't give a damn." I thanked him for his gift, and have often thought how kind he was, and how wise was his outlook on life.

After a wonderful year in England, we returned briefly to New York. I had been assigned to a Naval Medical Research Unit in Egypt and Kate, pregnant with our second child, spent the summer in Point Lookout while I went over to Cairo to begin my medical duties, find a home, and prepare it for my growing family.

The years based in Egypt may have been the most fortunate in our lives. Forced away from our own loving families in New York, deciding not to stay with the other Navy families in an almost incestuous American community in Cairo, we found our home and friends among the Arabs. We began to establish our own unique tastes. Kate learned to speak fluent Arabic, far better than I did. We had a three story house and a large, lush garden in Maadi, a suburb then separated by five miles of farm land from central Cairo; the villa cost 35 American dollars a month. We also had a beach cottage in Agame, outside Alexandria. The cottage had no running water or electricity, but it did have five acres of fig trees, a private beach on the Mediterranean, and we thought we had found paradise. The rent there was twelve American dollars a month, but with the added codicil that "if I was in residence," I had to deliver any and all children sired by Ali Mohamed, our landlord. During the next few years I successfully fulfilled the obstetrical requirements of the contract, delivering two healthy babies in the wadi next to our home.

Our cook, Marzouk, could prepare crepes suzettes on a Bunsen burner, and create elegant meals on an open charcoal fire. When Kevin's first birthday came we splurged hiring–for $38 per week–a private railroad car for a journey to Upper Egypt. We traveled with our cook and nanny, Kate's Uncle Gene and Aunt Betsy, and with Egyptian friends Kamel Wassef and his lovely daughter Nanice, to Luxor and Aswan. We met others on their own journey to peace, and profoundly appreciated our good karma. We also experienced, first hand, the nobility of the Islamic way of life.

There were periods when our national foreign policy–especially in relation to the ongoing and, as would be seen, endless Israeli-Palestinian crises–elicited, certainly in Cairo, popular, and sometimes violent, anti-American reaction. One night we received a telephone call from the US Embassy security staff urging us to stay indoors and remove anything that indicated our American identity. The Embassy informed us they could not guarantee our safety since our home was apart from the American compound. We did the best we could; closed the shutters, and kept our two young, innocent children in the bedroom with us.

At dawn I peeked through the window to see more than a dozen people on our lawn. One I recognized as a neighbor, a Colonel in the Egyptian army. I went outside urging them all to go away, for the spies from the Interior Ministry would come, as they often did even on peaceful days, at first light, and photograph anyone who was present. I argued with the Colonel that he was in particular danger of being identified, of being labeled as a collaborator, and surely losing his position. "But you cared for my daughter," he answered, "when she was horribly cut; you sewed up my girl's face, and let her smile. You are our guest and I will give my life for you and your family." We had never met people who would protect us with their lives. We were no longer transient visitors, tourists on the fly. We had been received as friends; those on the lawn were our hosts and, true to the Koran, would not abandon us if the mobs came. It all ended quietly, but we knew from then on we would be safe, not only in Egypt but wherever we traveled or lived in the Arab world.

Leaving our wedding reception, and facing, together, and with an almost unreasonable confidence in our future, a world for us of ever expanding options. When Kate died 44 years later I sat up at night noting that I had worked in humanitarian crises in 65 countries. I never took Kate into war zones or early disaster areas (such as after earthquakes), but on return assessment trips she had accompanied me to 45 refugee camps.

With Kate and our oldest son, Kevin, on the beach near our home outside Alexandria, Egypt. Most of the expatriate community had been expelled over the Suez crisis, and there were few neighbors. Our cottage had no running water or electricity, but it did have acres of fig trees and a rental cost of twelve American dollars per month.

Continuity

I think my Navy salary was $15,000 per year, yet it was more than ample for our needs. It was a period in Egypt when there were few tourists and most of the foreign residents (particularly English and French) had been expelled because of the Suez crisis. With Kate's exquisite taste we furnished a home with Oriental lamps and rugs, tombstones and old doors, Islamic chairs, couches, chests and even one of King Farouk's beds. We slowly put together an extensive library of rare books, early manuscripts, Korans, and Islamic, Turkish and Persian calligraphy. All were selected on the basis of their beauty. Only when we returned to New York, and had them reviewed by scholars, did we discover that most were of museum quality.

My work at the US Naval Medical Research Unit (NAMRU) was at first restricted to a well groomed six acre scientific campus of low white washed frame buildings housing some of the best laboratory equipment then existing in the Middle East. The main research US Navy projects there at the time were studies on the identification of tick species, an elaborate investigation on zinc metabolism in dwarfs, possibly the least important public health problem then facing a poor, disease-ridden nation. Adjacent to the NAMRU, but separated by a large gate with a rusted chain and lock, was a sprawling, dirty, sixty acre collection of 19th century stone buildings with tin roofs and broken windows. This was the Abassia Fever Hospital.

The Abassia Fever Hospital's tuberculosis meningitis building had seven adult males on cots in a room that might comfortably fit a bed, chair, and side table in a Western hospital. The shutters were closed to keep out the sun, but the side effect of this desire for shade was the lack of moving air, and in that stifling, dark setting patients survived–or died–cared for mostly by relatives and often without drugs or clean dressings.

There were buildings designated for tetanus patients, for anthrax, leishmaniasis, malaria as well as tuberculosis, meningitis and gastroenteritis; perforated typhoid cases had their own ward, and the large number of "fevers of unknown origin" were housed together, waiting, frequently without success before death intervened, for the disease to manifest itself clearly and make a specific diagnosis possible, a determination often painfully slow because of the lack of any laboratory facilities.

I asked permissions to establish cooperative programs with Abassia doctors, to use our laboratories to study and help their patients. My request was not encouraged ("It's never been done" being the only explanation from the tired Naval Commanding Officer (CO) completing his final tour of duty). But he did not forbid me to make contact. I broke the chain, pushed open the gate and began daily bedside clinical rounds with Egyptian colleagues.

Every day I would see diseases I had only read about, and, as is only possible with constant repetitive exposure to the varying clinical manifestation of illness, I became quite skilled in the diagnosis and therapy of these exotic infections. I began weekly lectures for our staff. This soon encouraged the CO to officially appoint me "Director of Clinical Tropical Medicine, and Chief of Epidemiology for Africa and the Middle East."

I had been given almost inordinate opportunity and responsibility at a very early age. Kate, commenting proudly on the title, said, "It can't get any better than this; it might all be downhill from here on." But it wasn't to be; it just got better, and better, as I began a two year exploratory journey studying the spread of epidemics, all through Egypt, out into the Western Desert, to Libya, down into the Delta, up the Nile to Luxor and Aswan, and then on to the Southern Sudan, Ethiopia, Somalia, Djibouti, Turkey, Lebanon, Iran and beyond. These surely were days "when the going was good."

One of my major scientific interests during this period was to study the accuracy, and practicality, of using rapid diagnostic tools in the midst of epidemics. Under diverse, difficult field conditions I worked with new immunologic methods to define the geographic spread of infectious outbreaks, thereby allowing scarce medical resources to be directed in the most restricted area. This was particularly crucial in developing lands where even basic public health programs were often nonexistent. An example of this approach was the use of a skin test for the leishmaniases, a group of parasitic diseases common throughout Africa and the Middle East. One major epidemic brought me to the Iraq/Turkish border.

Despite the fact that a successful national eradication program had largely eliminated the parasite in Turkey a few years earlier, the chaos that follows conflict and war is the fertile soil in which epidemics rekindle and flourish. Political turmoil in both Syria and Iraq had caused large numbers of Kurds to flee from still leishmanial infected areas into Turkey. The refugees brought with them a cutaneous form of the disease, and deep facial scars were disfiguring people all over southeastern Turkey. I was asked to direct an emergency epidemiologic and control program, with a field laboratory, surveillance and treatment teams.

A base was established in Diyarbakir, one of the few walled cities that withstood the onslaught of Genghis Khan. Our task was to identify the causative agent and try to contain the epidemic. I spent six weeks on horseback, protected by some fifty Turkish cavalrymen, on the steppes of the Tigris-Euphrates valley. We rode through historic hill towns–Urfa, Sirit, and around the shores of Lake Van–eating over open campfires and sleeping in the shadows of monuments in the home of civilization. We were able to localize and eradicate the epidemic by isolating infected towns, imposing a partial quarantine until aggressive drug administration had broken the cycle of transmission.

I returned to my family in Egypt full of wonder at–and gratitude for–the incredible privilege my profession provided. Money could not have brought these experiences, the instant, welcoming and warm access to people in distress. They greeted me not as a stranger or a tourist, but as one who had come to help and heal. They shared their homes and their culture, appreciating that medicine offers a universal foundation on which trust and love could almost always be quickly established.

Kate traveled separately (with her beloved Uncle Gene) to the great cities of Syria and Iraq, enriching our lives with experiences and memories that are reflected in furnishings and artwork in our homes. Quite regularly, at the end of the week's work, the remarkable American Ambassador to Egypt, John Badeau, one of John F. Kennedy's intellectual appointees, would call and ask what I was doing. If I wasn't involved in a critical experiment or sick patient, we would soon be off in the Embassy plane to Beirut, the "Paris of the East" for food, wine, poetry readings, picnics in Baalbak, Tripoli, Sidon and Tyre.

We also had long conversations on the very complex politics of the modern Middle East; Ambassador Badeau strongly encouraged my nascent interest in the potential of combining medicine and diplomacy. He would also advise me "to bring the attaché case." In Egypt we had to exchange American dollars for Egyptian piastres at a very low official rate. In Beirut's open currency market one got almost four times the Cairo rate. Our real salary quadrupled, and it was legal–or at least I was led to believe so by the good Ambassador. He remained a good friend, patient, and strong supporter, until he died many years later.

Of the many expeditions during my years at NAMRU two may best exemplify the profound and lasting impact Africa had on our life. My first intense period of prolonged loneliness was in the Southern Sudan. Caught behind battle lines in a conflict that still rages over fifty years later, I was there when the missionaries, who constituted the only health service in the area, were ejected. I found myself as the only physician in an area the size of New England. At night I would draw circles, speculating that I was the sole Caucasian in a radius of 300 miles, or maybe the only one with clothes in a 200 mile diameter. I wasn't off by much. I had inherited from the missionaries a wood burning, rear paddles steamer, and embarked on a journey of healing along the Nile. The course was through the Sudd, a choking swamp where, if the "captain" made the wrong turn, he told me the ship might well be trapped forever.

Not all work in tropical medicine takes place in warm climates. This photo is taken in the highlands of Ethiopia at the end of a months-long tour from Jig Jiga in the Ogaden and across to Gambela facing Sudan. The goal of the trip was to define opportunities for a U.S. Navy Medical Research Unit in advance of our almost certain ejection from Egypt due to the Israeli-Palestinian conflict, another early example of my immersion in the diplomatic implications of "scientific" studies.

I never miss the chance to read a good book. It was kept well wrapped in oil cloth and the text could then be retrieved and nourish my mind and soul in most unlikely places.

One day a "runner" arrived with a telegram that had been sent from Cairo two months earlier. It read: "Wife having miscarriage." The telegram had gonc from Cairo to Khartoum, but no one could get through the conflict zones to deliver it to me. I suspected that I might find some type of Morse code facility at a government station at the Ethiopian border some sixty miles away. I managed to find an outboard motor boat and went up the Sobat River, being shot at several times, once by a group on the promontory of Doleib Hill, a forsaken rise in the swamp where, on his great African journey after leaving the Presidency, Teddy Roosevelt almost died of malaria.

There was indeed a telegraph machine at the military base on the border; a cooperative officer, amazed that I had survived the hazardous trip through rebel territory, contacted the American Embassy in Addis Ababa, which was then able to reach our Embassy in Cairo. A diplomat there visited my wife, and reported, by return Morse code, that the miscarriage had only been a "threat." The baby survived and, fully healthy, saw his first light the next year in New York.

Life in the swamps of the Southern Sudan brought many lessons to a young doctor. I once ran a clinic in Fashoda, 600 miles south of Khartoum, where Marchard and Kitchener held their momentous meeting that carved up the colonial map, and the lives, of modern Africa. No one consulted the "natives"–they were naked and primitive and couldn't speak our language and didn't, until they were forced to, worship our God. But one only worked among the Shilluk and Nuer and Dinka for a short time before one realized they had retained their ancient crafts, and understood the ways of the river, and the beauty of the swamps, better than the white man could even imagine.

I found myself in situations that, for me at least, were without precedent. One quickly came to understand that tradition and culture were as essential as aspirin and bandages in running a rural medical program in the Sudan. One also quickly realized that prejudice and economic exploitation are realities that must be faced if one is to fulfill the obligations of a physician. It is necessary to appreciate the cry of the oppressed, the burden of ignorance, and fear and poverty, if one is to practice medicine in a developing land, especially during–and after–periods of chaos and disaster. There had been no lectures in the American medical school curriculum that would help me establish refugee camps. Our training in diagnosis and therapy had prepared one for a wellstocked consulting room, but not for the grand scale I now faced.

Solutions were discovered more frequently in the intellectual foundations of anthropology, Aristotelian logic and Thomistic reasoning, learned at Fordham College, than in the technical formulae of the sciences we had been taught in medical school. One learned to adapt on the spot, to be imaginative and flexible, and to try to develop life-saving programs built on an understanding and humility fostered in earlier courses in comparative religion and in the bitter lessons of history, even if one quickly realized that most of the history we had learned was biased to glorify Western achievements.

I had never considered how to construct a health service in the middle of a war, to do it with few supplies, and with only semiskilled "dressers." The "witch doctor" had a hold on the community, but his results left much to be desired. Does one fight such a system using the formidable forces of science and technology, or should one accommodate, abandoning that superior perch we have built from knowledge and training, in order to serve the suffering? I saw no alternative and we joined forces. He helped get me people to train and spread the word that my modern methods complemented his insights and skills.

There were experiences that tested the very core of a young doctor's soul. I recall staying up the first few nights after the missionary medical teams had gone into exile. I would deliver babies and sew up animal bites, try to dress fetid wounds and even amputate gangrenous limbs. But finally after two days, utterly exhausted, I said I was going to sleep, and I did. My Navy Corpsman assistant called me shortly thereafter to say a woman was bleeding; I got up to help and then again went back to bed. And again he called, but then I refused to get up. I said I couldn't survive if I didn't sleep and sent him away. I slept soundly for ten hours. I don't know to this day what ingredients–apart from sheer exhaustion–led to that decision. I recalled the lines of Yeats: "Too long a sacrifice/Can make a stone of the heart."

I began a daily routine of hard work, during the day organizing a basic health service, sharing the satisfying credit with my "witch doctor" friend, training volunteers in first aid, and going to sleep at night after a decent dinner of gazelle or quail. I stayed for over three months in the Southern Sudan and almost felt guilty realizing how much I enjoyed the bizarre experiences.

None of the doctors who replaced me stayed very long because they did not believe it was moral to leave the dying and go to bed. They felt that violated their Hippocratic Oath. They would nobly work until they fell, which they inevitably did in a matter of days. The program collapsed, the modern medical men went back to their laboratories and clinics, and the indigenous people to their own means and methods of survival. Who was right? Each must make their own decision, but I would make the same choice today as I did a half century ago.

As a part of my Navy epidemiology work I also traveled to Somalia, beginning a long love affair with the noble people and the harsh terrain of that forsaken land. I first went to the horn of Africa to investigate a diarrheal disease that was literally decimating an area hundreds of miles north of Mogadishu. With a microbiologist and technician we quickly determined the cause of the epidemic, a rare bacteria not previously known in Africa but sensitive to a common antibiotic. Excited by the discovery we made the long trek back to Mogadishu and, as a proper Navy Officer, went to the U.S. Embassy to tell them of our findings. We were told the Ambassador was too busy to see us–how one could be so busy in that sleepy capitol was mind boggling. But we had a deadly epidemic, and the solution on our hands. I went over to the World Health Organization (WHO) office, and provided the information to the doctor in charge. They made an international appeal for the curative drug, and China supplied enough to halt the outbreak. China was rewarded with the contract to build roads, a hospital and a stadium. It was an early–and never forgotten–lesson in the diplomatic implications of international medicine.

I continued my research work in Somalia by following camel herding nomads on their endless trek in search of water. Over the next ten years I walked the full length of that country, from top to bottom, and began to know Somali hospitality; they, who had so little, would share their food and camel's milk. They would have given their lives to protect me and, once again, I felt completely safe as I traveled the Somali bush with nomads and camels, lying at night under the open, star-filled sky, finding the Southern Cross and constellations before a peaceful sleep. I witnessed the strength of their ancient traditions, the songs and *gabays* of a beautiful people with ethnic pride, tribal support and strong religious foundations.

I made annual medical trips to Somalia for the next 35 consecutive years. I was there when the nation was born, and when it collapsed in the face of corruption, incompetence, international gamesmanship and the perverse forces of superpower politics. Nonetheless, when I reflect on the factors that fashion who I am and why, the isolation of the Somali landscape, and the courage and nobility of the nomad rank high. At least in part I am what I am because of them.

When I was young, and very innocent, I thought I was inordinately important as a medical doctor in a refugee camp. But it did not take long to realize, with growing humility, that those in charge of water, or food, or shelter, or security, or sanitation, or education were essential partners. Everyone in a field operation comes to appreciate that no one can accomplish very much working alone. If there was to be any progress in restoring a semblance of stability for those who had lost almost everything, we had to overcome our own restrictive professional barriers. Experiences often ran counter to the established didactic methods so easily accepted as doctrine in a Western medical school.

As but one important example, in delivering humanitarian assistance, one must learn to approach those in pain in a non-judgmental manner. Relief workers must leave behind their pride, their preconceptions, and sublimate their own interests and agendas in an act of solidarity with refugees and displaced persons. They must learn to tread softly, to offer change with great care. Existing customs and practice in any community, especially in the chaos of refugee camps, must not be altered without consultation and deliberation.

The ways of a people, sometimes quite incompressible to a person trained in a Western scientific system, are ultimately that group's own precious heritage and protection. Attempts to introduce new methods, and replace timeworn approaches can be devastating in times of crisis, when the utter failure of society makes people extremely vulnerable, while simultaneously forcing them to be completely dependent on strangers for the essentials of life.

I have been caught behind the lines in armed conflicts, and seen senseless slaughter from Beirut to Managua, and all across the scarred landscape of modern Africa. Somehow in the twisted wreckage of war, and in the squalor of refugee camps, the incredible beauty of humanity prevailed for me, as it does for most of those privileged to work in humanitarian assistance.

I learned that prejudice and economic exploitation, pride and politics, racism and religion, weather and witchcraft, corruptions and incompetence, were all integral parts of the problems I had to address. It was essential to hear, and appreciate, the cry of the oppressed, and the burden of ignorance, fear and poverty, if one was to be able to provide help in developing lands, especially during–and after–periods of disaster.

It was my privilege to serve, and even begin to identify with those caught in the crossfire conflicts not of their own making. A spiritual solidarity develops in just being with them. They were my brothers and sisters. I have always returned–although part of me never returned–from refugee camps gratified to be allowed to participate in their valiant efforts. I have helped, even healed, many desperate victims in humanitarian crises, but they in turn, helped, healed, instructed, and enriched me. It is that perspective that sustains us on what otherwise may seem like a journey through hell on earth. It takes time to refocus the romance of youth into reflective, lasting programs in humanitarian crises, to change the passion of love into healing projects.

Sometimes unusual circumstances occur that could result in bitter confrontation but may lead to understanding, ultimately to trust, and even love. Coming down in a hotel elevator in Addis Ababa, Ethiopia, I found myself the only Caucasian with a group of loud, angry American black men. They were talking of the wrongs that had been done to their people in our country, and said that they would never forget, and never forgive. Knowing their comments were pointed at me–since most comments began with "Whitey"–and, while accepting there was much justice to their assertions, especially in those pre-civil rights days, I, nonetheless, did not feel personally guilty. Silence would have been cowardly, so after the elevator stopped I turned and said, "You may not forget, but you must learn to forgive, to move beyond your hatreds." I stated that I was a young physician trying to help the oppressed people they presumed to speak for.

Later that night the leader of the group talked with me in the lobby of the hotel for a few hours. Neither of us completely convinced the other but I must have had some impact. The man was Malcolm X, the fiery and charismatic leader of the Black Nationalist movement of the time. Shortly after his return to America he was assassinated in Harlem. When I came back to New York, his widow, Betty 10X Shabazz, contacted my office asking for a medical appointment. Her husband had told her of our meeting and said that if she ever needed a "good and honest" doctor she should find me. That was a compliment from the grave that I treasured; I was able to return his trust and confidence with medical care. The widow remained my patient till she died, and two of her daughters still come to my office.

By the time we returned to New York, expecting our third child, we were our own independent selves, influenced not only by great and ancient art, rich and diverse experiences that provided a balance, a perspective, an almost unique foundation on which we would build our new life. We had seen terrible poverty, and famine and revolution, but also incredible beauty.

In my medical life I had changed utterly. I had discovered the satisfaction of condensing thoughts and arguments into cohesive lectures, of mixing the traditions of academia with a very active clinical practice, of exploring the boundaries of my discipline. Those satisfactions, that excitement, has blessedly stayed at that very high level all my professional life. The diverse titles and responsibilities I was to hold, both at home and abroad, have much of their foundation built in Africa and the Middle East.

I had learned not to shy away from challenges, no matter how large or new; not to limit, in any way, the options that emerged, not to place false restrictions in the search for solutions to apparently intractable problems. It would have certainly been safer to reap the rewards and stay within the expected confines of a predictable, standard modern medical career. But that was not what fate offered us. We had discovered each other, and our own way of life.

I also became convinced that being a physician did not preclude my being an observer–and should not prevent me from direct participation in politics and diplomacy. The more I worked in refugee camps, dealing with the multiple forces that influence humanitarian crises, it became very clear to me that answers often lay in disciplines beyond traditional medicine. In Africa, as I explored–in the field, at the bedside and in the laboratory–the root causes for individual diseases, I quickly discovered that the standard medical texts artificially constrained my understanding and appreciation of other factors equally important in epidemics.

It became ever more clear that identical pathogenic organisms produced very different diseases in hosts, influenced by, among other factors, age, nutrition, the cumulative effect of multiple infections, and medications. Even cultures influenced the epidemiology of disease; what one group of people might accept as normal another would report as illness. As I proceeded in my professional career, studying the origins and spread of infections, the more I came to appreciate–and admire–how scientific explorations became intertwined with forces we had simply never considered as part of medicine.

There were important personal factors that grew along with my official positions, resulting in decisions and actions affecting many thousands of unseen persons. How to stay true to my core values and basic philosophy was important to me in developing long term policies. The dangers of expediency were a constant challenge.

A small group of generous and wise advisors emerged, and informal confidential opinions were sought. The most important person was my wife, Kate. Although she had no training in medicine or public health she knew me best. If after hearing of a difficult decision she were to say "that doesn't sound like you, Kevin," I would reevaluate the approach. More often than not, she was correct in her assessment.

As one example of extending the definition of medicine, I had begun, in those early Navy years, to reflect on–and write about–the potential role of health and humanitarian assistance in international diplomacy. It seemed so obvious that a focus on these areas could allow a suspicious, skeptical and even hostile world to appreciate the caring, compassionate side of America. Over the next five decades, as I worked in more than 70 nations, primarily among refugees, with the poor and oppressed, in war zones and after natural disasters, these early ideas grew into firm convictions. Kate would sometimes claim I had become obsessed with making health and humanitarian issues central to our foreign policy rather than peripheral afterthoughts.

I wrote books and articles, even a Bill for the United States Congress (HR10042), promoting my theses with passion. Sometimes I succeeded but, as the ongoing wars of today sadly demonstrate, I failed to change the futile, militaristic mindset of too many of our leaders. But one can never stop trying–the cause of peace, of alleviating suffering, is simply too important to let our frustrations or disappointments drive us from the battle. Often I merely seemed to be waging an endless attack on elusive targets, tilting at the windmills of a hard life. And yet there were unexpected periods of progress and success, and some lasting rewards for having at least attempted to right wrongs in many desperate, forgotten corners of our world.

As I came to the end of my Cairo tour the reenlistment enticements offered by the Navy steadily increased with promises of a rapid rise in their research division. We loved working overseas, and "signed on" for another two years when I was offered command of a planned new NAMRU center in Addis Ababa, Ethiopia. Kate returned with our children to visit family and I undertook another exploratory mission through the country, doing a survey and feasibility study that went from the jungle areas near Gambella in the South, over to the desert towns of Dire Dawa and Jig Jiga, up through the highlands of Axum and Asmara, and down to the Red Sea ports. Several months later I ended up back in capital, met with their absolute ruler, whose remarkable title was "His Imperial Majesty, Haile Selassie I, Conquering Lion of the Tribe Judah, King of Kings and Elect of God" and was convinced that all was settled.

But when I returned to the States to report on our scientific journey at Naval Headquarters, I was informed that the Addis initiative would be delayed for at least one year. I had been reassigned to a research program in Washington, D.C. I argued vigorously with, (and I still recall his name because of his goodness and understanding) Captain Millar, Chief of Health Personnel, that I had extended only because we were promised we would remain in Africa.

At first he dismissed my complaints saying, "You don't sign contingency extensions with Uncle Sam." But the longer we talked the more he was persuaded of the justice of my argument. He finally offered to take the "extension sheet" out of my official "jacket" but said, "You must get out now as you're already overdue for discharge." These were Vietnam War days, and only his courageous and generous spirit allowed me to escape a long military career.

I called Kate from a phone booth in the street outside Naval Headquarters and, without a job but with full confidence, we were back in civilian life, in our home town, New York, and we were ready to start another phase of our lives.

I first went to Yemen in the early 1960's to investigate a suspected outbreak of small pox in the Egyptian forces trying to overthrow the ruling Imam. In the years ahead I made many epidemiological field trips, collecting specimens for serologic surveys of tropical diseases in this often closed society. Medicine would open doors and provide a common ground for trust and friendship throughout the world.

Unity and Diversity

My wife wrote many poems about our love; one cited here captures her literary talent as well as the definition of our marriage.

Strange it is and lovely
How two lives intermingle
And tread upon the
Dreams that both have known–

Dreams fulfilled and
Those tested
Yet clasped and held as one.

This final section of *Labyrinths* is presented in that spirit–an appreciation how multiple projects that would have been considered full careers in most biographies have been mysteriously, as with love, linked. Rather than being distinct and separate activities, they were accepted as part of a full professional life where false barriers were avoided, and a common philosophy allowed one to address different challenges simultaneously, drawing strength from the influences and experiences considered in earlier sections of this book. There was unity in diversity. If a labyrinth suggests mystery, the topics and themes considered here offer, I hope, answers to difficult, sometimes intractable, problems, and can help guide us out of the maze.

Since most of the parts reviewed in this section here have been already published as individual books or Occasional Papers, I will provide only brief introductions with visual images of relevant title pages. All books are available on the internet in both print and digital form.

Somalia & Nicaragua

Although I have participated in relief operations in over 70 countries two main areas of interest may best indicate the range of activities in field operations. I initially worked in Somalia as a young physician in the US Navy Research Unit investigating a fatal epidemic of dysentery in the early 1960s. My last visit just four years ago, was as one of three members of a high level United Nations team, including the President of the General Assembly and the Secretary General of the Organization.

During those 50 plus years, often with semi-annual trips to the Horn of Africa, I undertook extensive research projects defining disease patterns among the camel herding nomads, participated in relief missions after droughts and famines, organized large refugee camps, developed rehabilitation programs for victims of landmines, and served as a link with many government officials from Prime Ministers, Presidents, opposition political activists and diplomats.

The Tropical Disease Center (TDC) at Lenox Hill Hospital published a *Directory of Somali Professionals* a compendium of educated personnel from the diaspora willing to serve in various specialties. The Directory was a yearlong effort by a former Prime Minister, former Ambassador, and myself at the TDC, as an effort to encourage foreign governments and international aid agencies to hire Somalis rather than expatriates. While this project ultimately failed as the country spiraled into chaos during the 1990s, the concept is now generally embraced by the international aid world.

The Somali aspect of a major New York exhibit at Lenox Hill Hospital is largely based upon my own published books, research articles, public policy opinion papers, and presents art and artifacts acquired on these journeys. Somalia's culture is, primarily, an oral one. When I first went to the Horn there was no written language and traditions were passed through generations by poems and stories.

A poem by Mohammed Abdile Hassan, the national hero of Somalia, captures why I was accepted into a closed society:

Who welcomes you like a kinsman
in your day of need
and who at the height of the
drought
does not bar his gate against
you–
Is not he who never fails you in
your weakness one of your
brethren?

In Nicaragua I headed the health service after the earthquake in 1972 and have since helped provide medical and diplomatic support throughout the country, and over the decades, for an oppressed people and beleaguered nation.

For further reading:

Health on the Horn of Africa Spottiswoode, 1969
Somalia: A Perspective NYS University Press, 1980
Disaster in Nicaragua US Congressional Record, 1972

Ireland

For 36 years I served as Chairman of the Department of Tropical Medicine and International Health at the Royal College of Surgeons in Ireland (RCSI). During that period I taught over 4000 medical students from all over Europe, and developed multiple graduate programs for advanced degrees. The details of the RCSI experience can be found in *A Dream For Dublin, The Open Door* and *Irish Essays*. Now the longest serving full Professor in the 230 year history of the College, I am the recipient of Ireland's highest honor, the Presidential Medal. I also serve as Uachtarain of Cumann-Luachra (the President of a local historical society in County Kerry). For 40 years I was also the President-General of the American Irish Historical Society.

For further reading:

Irish Essays John Jay Pr., 1980
The Open Door R.C.S.I., 1999, 2014
A Dream For Dublin Northwell University Press, 2016

Government Positions

Although the primary focus of my professional life has been in overseas work in humanitarian assistance after disasters and conflicts, I have had the privilege of directing large scale health programs at the State and City level in New York.

For six years I was in charge of health and mental health in New York State with 80,000 employees reporting to me, and an annual budget of eight billion dollars. For the succeeding twelve years I served as the Senior Member of the New York City Board of Health. The details of these programs are available in the books cited below.

After the attack of 9/11/2001 I was appointed as the Chief Medical Advisor for Counterterrorism for the New York Police Department and served in that role for fifteen years. Although the main focus after the terrorist attack was on the collapse of the World Trade Center, the use of weaponized anthrax powder posed significant bioterrorist threats, at one point closing the U.S. Supreme Court, the House of Representatives and several major media headquarters.

For further reading:

Health in New York State Health Education Services, 1977
Imminent Peril Twentieth Century Fund, 1991
An Unfinished Tapestry Northwell University Press, 2015

Missionaries & Church

After completing my Navy service in the mid 1960s I returned to New York, and was soon overwhelmed by missionaries of all denominations. At that time few missionaries had any medical insurance. They returned from their field assignments after many years, and with many predictable, but undiagnosed, illnesses. With the generous help of Lenox Hill Hospital physician volunteers, we soon established a comprehensive health program. By the mid 1970s our missionary programs at Lenox Hill Hospital had examined and treated over seven thousand priests, nuns and religious volunteers of all denominations. We also studied missionaries as "sentinel" populations for epidemiologic research to determine what Americans might experience in disease exposure if they lived for prolonged periods in remote areas of the world. A more detailed report on this program is included in an Occasional Paper published in 2018.

After an assassination attempt in 1981 on His Holiness, Pope John Paul II, I was appointed as part of an emergency response team providing medical care. I never gave an interview, or wrote about that experience because of my deep belief in medical professional confidentiality. The one exception was when the Vatican asked me to submit to them some brief posthumous comments for their publication. I remained in close, personal and professional contact with His Holiness for many years. I served as his Personal Representative on a dangerous Pontifical Mission to war-torn Lebanon in 1982.

For further reading:

Missionary Influences: A Personal Tale Fordham University, 2018
A Pontifical Mission: Lebanon 1982 Fordham University, 2019

United Nations

For many decades I have served as a consultant in Tropical Medicine for the United Nations Medical Service. In the early years, I directed weekly clinics at the United Nations Headquarters but eventually coordinated this activity with the Tropical Disease Center at Lenox Hill Hospital.

I have served as Chief Advisor of Humanitarian Affairs and Public Health for three Presidents of the United Nations General Assembly, and for the United Nations Alliance of Civilizations. I led a United Nations Mission to Gaza after the Israeli invasion in 2009. I have trained hundreds of United Nations and Agency (WTF, UNRWA, UNICEF, UNMIL, WHO, IOM, UNOPS, UNOCHA, UNFPA, UN Women, WFP, and UNDP) staffs in our International Diploma in Humanitarian Assistance programs.

For further reading:

Gaza: Destruction and Hope UN Report, 2009
History and Hope: The International Humanitarian Reader Fordham University Press, 2013

My early interest in the diplomatic implications of tropical medicine began in Somalia. Later I could be involved, as a citizen, in the Vietnam War period when many Americans were seeking ways to emphasize the caring and compassionate side of a nation that seemed to have lost its focus. An Irish artist, after watching a Fourth of July parade in our tiny hamlet of Point Lookout, drew a picture of an American flag with the "heart in the stars," offering a valid alternative to our usual militaristic image.

I traveled to Cuba for many years, working in a leprosy hospital, and meeting colleagues through their world renowned Tropical Disease Institute, eventually being named as the only Honorary Member of the Cuban Microbiology Society. I also had the opportunity to share thoughts with their leaders, including numerous all night, wide ranging conversations with President Fidel Castro.

Coalescing

It is tempting to focus on activities in defining the multiple facets of a life spent on the front lines of tropical medicine and humanitarian relief work.The details of programs are obviously an important criteria but, ultimately, they are based on ideas; in fact, in a professional life, ideas matter most.

One concept that has permeated my entire career has been the conviction that the methodology of public health and even the semantics of medicine could be beneficially applied to the softer discipline of diplomatic dialogue.The missed opportunities for the United States in my early work in Somalia were never forgotten. I became increasingly committed, as a citizen, to not limit my attention merely to the diagnosis and treatment of illnesses. Gradually a cohesive philosophy of preventive diplomacy became central in my writings, and some senior, very respected statesmen promoted my ideas in this field.

In an interview shortly before his death at 93, former Secretary General of the United Nations Boutros Boutros Ghali was asked what he thought would be his most lasting legacy. He responded: "My work with Dr. Cahill in the mid1990's on preventive diplomacy." In his retirement, former U.S. Secretary of State, Cyrus Vance, expressed similar feelings.

For further reading;

A Bridge to Peace Haymarket Doyma, 1988
Preventive Diplomacy Basic Books, 1996, 2000
To Bear Witness: A Journey of Healing and Solidarity Fordham University Press, 2005, 2013

I conclude these reflections with an image, and a request. In providing relief after disasters we deal with the most vulnerable, those who have lost almost everything. We are partners in an ongoing struggle and must recognize the important roles each contributes. The image of a bridge is offered as a blend of poetry and practicality. By harnessing tensions and forces, we can span abysses, link separate lands, and create a structure of beauty. But soaring girders and grateful arches must be firmly anchored in a solid foundation lest a load of unplanned aspirations cause a collapse, destroying both bridge and travelers on the dangerous but wonder-filled journey of life. My request is that the reader try to absorb–and identify, if possible, with–my memories; as the Irish poet Yeats asked, "Tread softly, because you tread on my dreams."

For further reading;

Milestones in Humanitarian Action Fordham University Press, 2017

Books by Kevin M. Cahill, M.D.

Tropical Diseases in Temperate Climates
Health on the Horn of Africa
The Untapped Resource: Medicine & Diplomacy
Teaching Tropical Medicine
Health and Development
A Bridge to Peace
Tropical Diseases: A Handbook for Practitioners
Medical Advice for the Traveler
Irish Essays
Health In New York State: A Progress Report
Imminent Peril: Public Health in a Declining Economy
Threads for a Tapestry
Somalia: A Perspective
Famine
The AIDS Epidemic
The American-Irish Revival
Pets and Your Health
Directory of Somali Professionals
Clearing the Fields: Solutions to the Global Land Mines Crisis
Silent Witnesses
The Open Door: Health and Foreign Policy at the RCSI
A Framework for Survival
Preventive Diplomacy: Stopping Wars Before They Start
Basics of International Humanitarian Missions
Emergency Relief Operations
Traditions, Values, and Humanitarian Action
Human Security for All
Technology for Humanitarian Action
The Pulse of Humanitarian Assistance
The Open Door: Art and Foreign Policy at the RCSI
History and Hope: The International Humanitarian Reader

Tropical Medicine: A Clinical Text (Jubilee Edition)
Even in Chaos: Education in Times of Emergency
More with Less: Disasters in an Era of Diminishing Resources
To Bear Witness: A Journey of Healing and Solidarity
An Unfinished Tapestry
A Dream for Dublin
Milestones in Humanitarian Action
Medicine Tropicale

Cahill Occasional Papers

The Future of Somalia: Stateless and Tragic (with A.A. Farah, A.H. Hussein, and D. Shinn)
The University and Humanitarian Action
Romance and Reality in Humanitarian Action
Gaza: Destruction and Hope
Maharishi University Convocation
Missionary Influences
A Pontifical Mission: Lebanon 1982

*Many of the books are available in French translation. Some have been translated into Spanish, Italian, Portuguese, Arabic, Japanese, and other languages.

About the Center For International Humanitarian Cooperation

The copyright for this book has been transferred to the Center for International Humanitarian Cooperation (CIHC) and allows royalties to go directly towards the training of humanitarian workers. The CIHC is a U.S. Registered Public Charity that was founded in 1992 to promote healing and peace in countries shattered by natural disasters, armed conflicts, and ethnic violence. The Center employs its resources and unique personal contacts to stimulate interest in humanitarian issues and to promote innovative educational programs and training models. Our extensive list of publications and regular symposia address both the basic issues, and the emerging challenges, of international humanitarian assistance.

Since 2001, the CIHC has supported training in humanitarian activities through the Institute of International Humanitarian Affairs (IIHA) at Fordham University; it has now graduated over 3,000 humanitarian aid professionals from 140 nations, and continues to offer programs in Europe, Asia, Africa, Latin America and North America. The CIHC has formal partnerships with The Royal College of Surgeons in Ireland, University College Dublin, the NOHA network of European universities, United Nations World Food Programme (WFP), International Organization of Migration (IOM), International Medical Corps (IMC), Action Contre la Faim (ACF), Jesuit Refugee Service (JRS), the British Ministry of Defense, and other UN, NGO and governmental organizations.
The IIHA also offers Master Degrees as well as an undergraduate Major in humanitarian affairs.

Support the CIHC

With your donation we provide courses, trainings, and symposia, offering dozens of scholarships to students from the Global South, and conducting ongoing research and publications to promote best practices in humanitarian affairs. Please consider a recurring gift.

Donate online through our secure payment processor at:
www.cihc.org/support
You can also mail your gift to CIHC at:
850 Fifth Avenue, New York, NY 10065

We also accept donations of airlines miles, investments, bequests, etc.
Please contact us at mail@cihc.org or (212)-636-6294 to discuss.

About the Refuge Press

This is thc inaugural book published by a new imprint, The Refuge Press; it continues the International Humanitarian Book Series (IHA) and is distributed by Fordham University Press.The IHA Series has published 13 volumes on various aspects of providing relief in complex humanitarian crises.The IHA texts are widely used in universities and training programs around the world and have been translated into numerous languages.They are available in print and digital form.
Occasional Papers complement the books on specific historical topics.

About the Author

Kevin M. Cahill, M.D., is University Professor and Director of the Institute of International Humanitarian Affairs at Fordham University, President of the Center for International Humanitarian Cooperation, Professor of Clinical Tropical Medicine and Molecular Parasitology at New York University, Director of the Tropical Disease Center at Lenox Hill Hospital, Professor of International Health of the Royal College of Surgeons in Ireland, and completed a 15 year term as Chief Medical Advisor for Counterterrorism for the New York Police Department (NYPD). His career in tropical medicine and humanitarian operations began in Calcutta in 1959; he has carried out medical, relief and epidemiologic research in Africa, Latin America, and Asia. Dr. Cahill has written or edited 33 books, translated into many languages, and more than 200 articles in peer-reviewed journals on a wide range of subjects including infectious diseases, health and humanitarian assistance, foreign affairs, Irish history and literature. He holds numerous Honorary Fellowships and distinguished awards from foreign governments, and has received dozens of Honorary Doctorates from universities around the world.

Milton Keynes UK
Ingram Content Group UK Ltd.
UKHW020619120424
441015UK00004B/214